MY FIRST LOOK AT INSECTS

AN ANT CARRYING A BIG LEAF

Ants

TERESA WIMMER

CREATIVE EDUCATION

Published by Creative Education

123 South Broad Street, Mankato, Minnesota 56001

Creative Education is an imprint of The Creative Company

Designed by Rita Marshall

Photographs by Getty Images (Tim Flach, George Grall, David Maitland, Walter Meayers

Edwards, Andrew Mounter, Dean Riggott, Darren Robb, Kevin Schafer)

Printed in the United States of America

Library of Congress Cataloging-in-Publication Data

Wimmer, Teresa. Ants / by Teresa Wimmer.

p. cm. — (My first look at insects)

Includes index.

ISBN-13 : 978-1-58341-453-8

I. Ants—Juvenile literature. I. Title. II. My first look at insects.

QL568.F7W66 2006   595.79'6—dc22   2005037236

First edition 9 8 7 6 5 4 3 2 1

ANTS

SMALL AND STRONG

Lift up a rock, and a family of ants might be crawling there. Ants are small **insects**. They have six legs. Their legs are strong. They help the ants carry big loads such as sticks and other insects.

Ants do not have ears or a nose. They have feelers called **antennae** on the top of their head. Their antennae let them hear, smell, and touch things. Ants talk by tapping their antennae together.

ANTS CARRY STICKS BIGGER THAN THEMSELVES

Most ants eat plants and other insects. But they cannot chew whole food. Instead, they use their mouth to squeeze the juice from their food.

Ants are very strong.

They can lift 20 times

their own body weight.

Building a Home

Most ants live in nests. Many ants build their nests in the dirt. They dig **tunnels** and small rooms in the dirt.

Some ants use trees to build nests. At night, leaf-cutter ants cut pieces of leaves from trees. They put the leaves in their underground nest. Black carpenter ants build their nests in old logs or tree trunks.

Each ant **colony** has it own
smell. Ants know "strangers"
because they smell different.

SOME ANTS MAKE NESTS IN SAND

A few ants do not build nests at all. During the day, army ants march in long lines looking for food. At night, they hold on to each other and hang from a log.

A Big Family

Most ants do not like to be alone. They live together in colonies. There can be hundreds, thousands, or even millions of ants living in a colony.

A COLONY OF ANTS WORKING TOGETHER

The ants in a colony each do a different job. The queen ant lays eggs. Soldier ants protect the colony. They use their head to block the doorway of the nest. This keeps out spiders and insects that try to hurt the colony.

Worker ants build nests and look for food. When a worker ant finds food, it leaves a trail on the ground. The trail has a special smell. Other ants follow the trail to the food.

ANTS LIKE TO BE NEAR EACH OTHER

LITTLE HELPERS

Some people try to get rid of ants. But ants help other living things grow. Ants eat insects that hurt plants. The tunnels they dig mix up the dirt. The mixed-up dirt helps plants grow strong.

Some animals need ants to live. **Anteaters** can eat only ants. Frogs, toads, and lizards like to eat ants, too. Sometimes beetles and crickets like to live inside empty ant nests.

Anthills can be five feet
(1.5 m) high. That is almost
as tall as a grown-up!

AN "ANT BRIDGE" BETWEEN TWO LEAVES

Ants can be fun to watch. Many people keep ant farms in their homes. An ant farm is a clear jar or box filled with dirt and ants. People can watch the ants and learn how they live!

ANTS ARE VERY BUSY INSECTS

Hands-on: Ant Watching

Ants are big eaters. You can put out food and watch the ants come to eat it.

What You Need

One slice of bread, cut up in pieces
One cup (240 ml) of water in a bowl
Two teaspoons of sugar

What You Do

1. Put the sugar into the water. Stir the water for five minutes.
2. Soak the bread in the sugar water for a little while.
3. Put pieces of the bread in different places in your yard.
4. Check the bread every half hour to see how long it takes the ants to find it.
5. Watch the ants enjoy their feast!

AN ANT CLIMBING ON A FLOWER

Index

Words to Know

anteaters—big, hairy animals with long noses and no teeth; they eat only ants

antennae—long rods used by ants for feeling, smelling, tasting, and hearing

colony—a group of animals that live and work together

insects—small animals that have six legs

tunnels—underground "roads"

Read More

Brenner, Barbara. *Thinking About Ants*. Greenvale, N.Y.: Mondo Publishing, 1997.

Demuth, Patricia Brennan. *Those Amazing Ants*. New York: Macmillan Publishing, 1994.

Hodge, Deborah. *Ants*. New York: Kids Can Press, 2004.

Explore the Web

Amazing Active Ants http://www.maineanimalcoalition.org/artman/publish/article_204.shtml

Enchanted Learning.com http://zoomschool.com/subjects/insects/ant

The World of Our Little Friends, the Ants http://www.harunyahya.com/kids/theants1.html